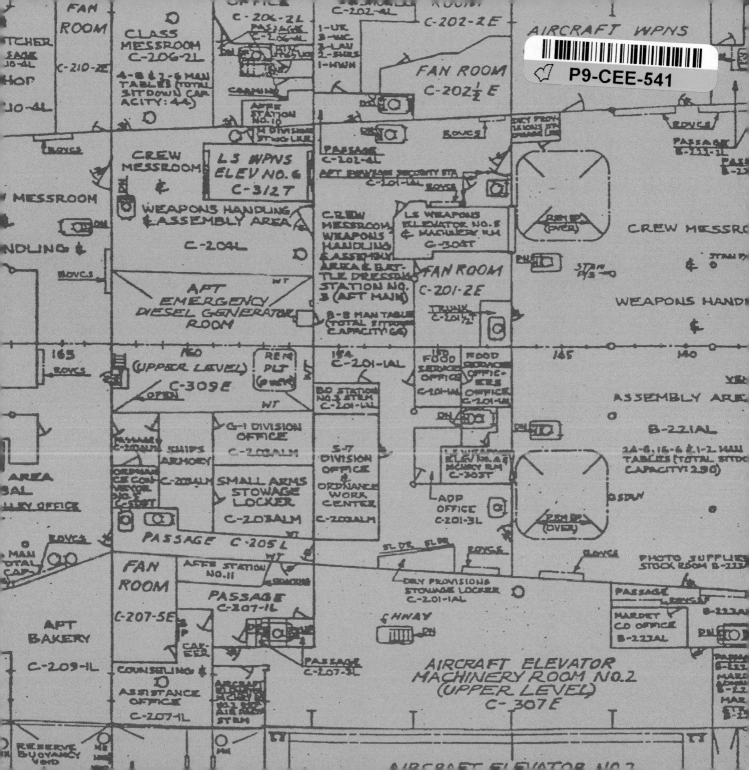

KARAS

MIDWAY MEMORIES

THE OFFICIAL PHOTO COLLECTION OF THE SAN DIEGO AIRCRAFT CARRIER MUSEUM

Scott McGaugh – Rudy Shappee

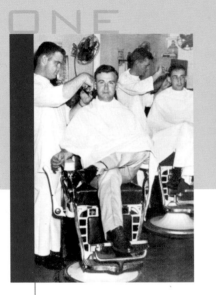

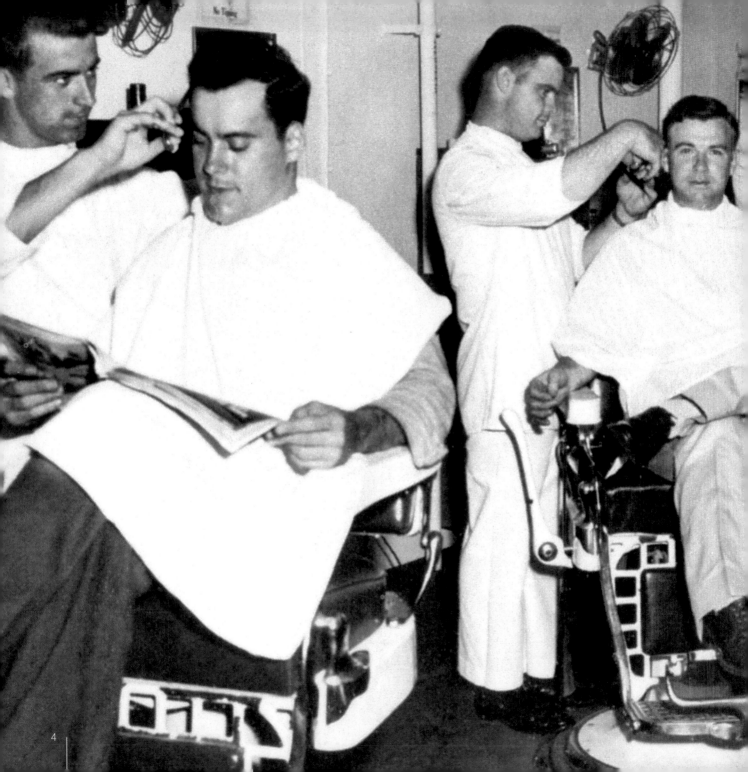

CHAPTER ONE

Midway's barbers gave
more than 13,000 haircuts
every month as sailors
were expected to get a
trim every 10 days.

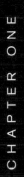

CITY AT SEA

Imagine a small town of 4,500 residents on a Kansas prairie. Everything found in that town—power plants, libraries, jail, restaurants, a hospital, electricians, tailors and storekeepers—was aboard the USS Midway, a floating city at sea. During nearly five decades of service from the 1940s to the 1990s, Midway and her crew were a unique microcosm of America, thousands of miles removed from her nation's shores.

She was a city at sea comprised of dozens of neighborhoods. Men assigned as boiler tenders and engine men slept, ate, and played cards only a few yards from their duty stations deep inside the ship. They lived in their "neighborhood" day in and day out, rarely leaving. A man didn't explore Midway on a lark. He lived and worked with a handful of other men assigned to similar jobs. As a result, loyalty often began with the man in the bunk above or below him and then radiated out to all that was Midway Magic.

In effect, Midway's captain was the mayor of this seagoing municipality. It was his job to meld individual neighborhoods of cooks, pilots, storekeepers, mechanics and welders into a cohesive force. If Midway hadn't functioned effectively as a city, she couldn't possibly have answered the call of the nation.

The C-1 Carrier Onboard Delivery aircraft sits proudly among the museum's fighting aircraft.

MEMORIES FROM HOME

A Midway sailor considered a letter from home more valuable than gold. In an era before sailors' personal email accounts, a Midway crewman sometimes waited weeks for a card or anything that might connect him to friends and family halfway around the world. The sight of a COD (Carrier Onboard Delivery) aircraft, laden with letters and packages from girlfriends, mothers and wives was a joy. Some packages were marked "Midway Majutsu" (meaning Magic).

Sailors frequently faced long lines at the ship's post office as they waited to send packages filled with exotic gifts home to friends and loved ones.

Distributing mail to 4,500 officers and crew aboard Midway required an eye for detail and a knack for keeping things organized.

Many Midway sailors
purchased money orders
at Midway's post office
and then sent them home
to help their families
make ends meet.

U. S. S. MIDWAY

11 January 1948

My Darling Wife:

Hello Darling its another Sunday
have is time on my hands, but I'll
it to a good purpose, and thats writing
This will be kind of hard as news is
I'll do my best.

To start with here a little in
don't know how true it is, but it
kind of log
in Hampton
ship will un
Navy Yard.
will be flown
I would ral
they will ke

Smiley ☺

I got your letter this morning
Thanks a lot. I love your
so much ☺ That letter is
Ive ever got
o much love be
feel now. (smi
g about you
missed you
g back today
you
y English
expres m
tape
ch.

ley ☺

UNITED STATES NAVY 8 Dec. 1947

My Darling:

Hello Sweetheart I am about
my favorite pastime and thats
to you.
I didn't write yesterday afternoon
said I would in my morning
was almost an impossibility.
darn English Sailors and civilians
all over the ship and I couldn't
o'clock as I had to go on watch
I got off watch I went to the
But anyway Darling I manage
te a little every day. By the way
all my people xmas cards except
lay and Elmer. I also sent one
Elsie & Jimmie. And I sent several
to you and another to your mom and
mine. Now don't I spread Christmas
cheer. I think you are going to like the

Ralph R. Robert aomm
U.S.S Midway (VF18)
% F.P.O. New York City
New York

U.S. MAIL
DEC
10
1947
CVB 42

VIA AIR MAIL

Mrs. Ralph R. Robert
% Mrs. O. E.

USS MIDWAY
MAJUTSU

7

BEEF STEW RECIPE
Yields: 2,000, 1-1/4 cup portions

- 600 lbs. Beef, diced, thawed
- 16 lbs. Flour, wheat, sifted
- 2 1/2 lbs. Salt
- 8 oz. Black pepper
- 8 oz. Dehydrated garlic
- 20 lbs. Melted shortening

Dredge beef in mixture of flour, salt, pepper and garlic. Shake off excess. Brown beef in hot shortening in steam-jacketed kettle.

- 50 gals. Hot water
- 100 #10 cans Canned crushed tomatoes
- 20 tbsp. Thyme
- 80 Bay leaves

Add water, tomatoes, thyme and bay leaves to meat. Cover; simmer 2 hours.

- 160 lbs. Carrots, fresh, 1/2-inch rings

Add carrots to beef mixture. Cover; simmer 15 minutes.

- 80 lbs. Celery, fresh, 1-inch pieces
- 24 lbs. Dry onions, in quarters
- 200 lbs. White potatoes, peeled, in pieces
- 2 1/2 lbs. Salt
- 20 lbs. Flour, wheat, sifted
- 20 gals. Cold water

Add celery, onions, potatoes and salt. Stir to mix. Cover; simmer 20 minutes or until vegetables are tender. Remove bay leaves. Thicken gravy, if desired. Combine flour and water. Add to stew while stirring. Cook 5 minutes, or until thickened.

13,500 MEALS A DAY

"No matter where Midway was on the world's oceans, it seemed the lines to get food always extended to Spain." Chow and plenty of it kept a Midway sailor going. Six galleys aboard Midway operated nearly 24 hours a day, 7 days a week. It was a brutal regimen of preparing 4 meals a day, including "mid-rats" (midnight rations) so men working through the night could eat. Then it was four hours of cleaning and restocking before the grills and griddles were fired up again in a relentless routine of heat, steam and sweat.

The Navy's famous bean soup was prepared in these massive 50-gallon steam kettles.

To celebrate the 60,000th landing aboard Midway in 1953, the largest cake known to have ever been baked on the carrier, measuring 24 feet in length, was served.

Every night Midway bakers baked as many as 1,000 loaves of bread. Then day crews took over the galleys, filling ovens with beef roasts, hams and Christmas turkeys.

"Flat cakes" on Midway were a staple. They were served at breakfast, sprinkled with sugar and cinnamon. After dinner they were considered dessert when covered with icing.

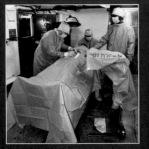

Major surgeries were conducted at sea in Midway's sick bay.

There were 18 berths in sick bay and three more in the ship's intensive care unit.

Museum visitors can explore sick bay and its ongoing restoration.

Hundreds of prescriptions a day could be filled at the ship's pharmacy.

SHOTS AND SPLINTS

Break a leg? See the ship's surgeon. Lose a filling? The dentist's office was next door. A complete medical complex aboard Midway tended to most sailors' needs, from wounds to illness, from a toothache to an impacted molar. Vicious scrapes from the non-skid flight deck, cracked shins from tripping over tie-down chains, and minor concussions from walking into an aircraft on a darkened hangar deck kept the medical staff busy. Sick bay included an intensive care unit and x-ray rooms. Of course, tattoo removal and medications for certain "communicable" diseases were available as well.

Midway sailors had to be inoculated before arrival in foreign ports where they might be exposed to cholera or the plague.

Midway's dental staff took care of more than 140,000 teeth in an endless series of cleanings, x-rays and fillings.

ALL THE NEWS

Like any small town, the USS Midway had a fully equipped print shop and newspaper staff. Early editions of Midway News were mimeographed. Later mimeographs were replaced by lead type printing presses and then by computerized layouts. The ship's newspaper usually was published weekly. Most issues reflected the interests of the crew: highlights from outdated newspapers flown aboard Midway; staid reports from department heads; the latest standings in the shipboard basketball tournament; a crossword puzzle; and a photo of a Hollywood B-actress modeling the latest in swimsuit fashion. Sometimes articles caught the crew by surprise such as the day in 1953 when Midway broadsided a wayward whale in the Mediterranean.

Midway's print shop today is quiet, ready for restoration and opening to the public.

Sometimes the print shop produced classified publications only for the crew's use.

WMID IS ON THE AIR

Midway's theme song in the 1980s was "Fanfare for the Common Man," written by Aaron Copland.

Music soothed the soul aboard Midway. While the ship's volunteer radio "personalities" may not have been as polished as Wolfman Jack, they provided a steady stream of music spanning Jerry Lee Lewis to Bon Jovi. Sailors could listen to a nearby speaker or wrap a wire around it, connect it to their personal radio's FM band, and tune in to WMID. The format varied from hour to hour, based on the interests of the DJ on duty. It often was an eclectic blend of music and musicians, prompting one listener to remark, "Most everyone on Midway liked at least some of the music, some of the time."

LIVE ON KMID

For a few hours each day, Midway's televisions located in scattered nests of berths and bunks flickered to life when KMID went on the air. Sailors looked forward to this diversion during off-duty hours, whether it was watching 1951's A Streetcar Named Desire or 1991's Terminator 2: Judgment Day. Other times, a Midway sailor dressed in a suit and tie stiffly read the news relayed from Midway's teletype only minutes before. Some sailors saw Midway's skipper only on "Captain's Call" when the carrier's senior officer alternatively informed and encouraged his crew. One day, a skipper famous for his sense of humor was visibly flustered when a streaker, clad only in a mask, raced across the TV screen during the captain's live broadcast.

Several network television programs were filmed aboard Midway, including On Your Account in 1954.

Specialists check a film splice prior to showing a movie on the ship's television system.

COBBLERS, TAILORS & LIBRARIANS

"What did you do on Midway, Daddy?" "Son, I worked in the geedunk." "I resoled shoes." "I sewed buttons on shirts and repaired flags." "I was in charge of the 3,000 books in the library." "I kept an eye on the brig's inmates." As a city at sea, sailors anonymously toiled in many of Midway's 2,000 compartments. Some were as oblivious to flight ops as they were unknown to the men who flew above the clouds. Yet they were equally important in ensuring that the nation could count on Midway Magic to fulfill every mission. The ship set a record in 1973 by being at sea for 327 consecutive days.

Midway's brig enabled swift, at-sea justice and meaningful punishment for deserving sailors and Marines.

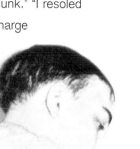

Seven ship's stores on Midway offered a wide array of items, ranging from razor blades to Rolex® watches.

CHAPTER TWO

A signalman sends
a message to one of
the ships in Midway's
task group.

BURDEN OF COMMAND

More than 4,000 young men, most of them barely out of their teens
and away from home for the first time, counted on the officers who
commanded them. These officers held the President's commission
and were responsible for ensuring that young sailors made jet engine
replacement parts to incredibly fine tolerances. They made sure young
men operated the catapult precisely so that just the right amount of
steam pressure drove each individually weighed aircraft off the bow.
They trained sailors to don fire suits and lumber into flight deck
infernos on the slim chance a pilot's life could be saved. The burden
of commanding these young men was both draining and exhilarating.
Former captains of Midway routinely called their command of the
nation's longest-serving carrier the highlight of their career. And with
good reason...

COMMANDING 4,500 MEN

A man lives in another dimension when he has command of an American aircraft carrier. The U.S. Navy has only a handful of such openings for a job wrought with incomprehensible risk and reward. As Midway patrolled the seas or steamed toward an engagement, captains were never off duty. They slept on a fold-out couch only 10 steps from the bridge, high in the island. Most counted it a blessing if they got two to three uninterrupted hours of sleep a night. There were an infinite number of variables and untold consequences at stake when a man and his department heads commanded the USS Midway. Thousands of sailors depended on them for insightful decisions. Millions of Americans relied on their instincts and professionalism. The demands placed on them exacted a heavy toll on men who lived in officers country.

High atop the flight deck, the island was the command nerve center of Midway and its task group.

Communicating commands to Midway's crew was an important part of the commanding officer's job.

Many decisions required department head and division officer input. Everyone lived with the constant pressure of providing the most current and complete information to Midway's commanding officer.

PRI-FLY

He was called the Air Boss. Many considered his job of commanding primary flight control on Midway to be the most demanding and thankless responsibility on the ship. Pri-fly was the essence of Midway's existence. It was responsible for all flight deck launch and recovery operations. High above the flight deck, the Air Boss often had four radios draped on his head, shoulders, and chest as he constantly communicated with men on the flight deck and inbound pilots "in the groove."

Aircraft launches and recoveries occurred every minute, leaving no room for error, no room for doubt. Second guessing sometimes came at the cost of a man's life. The plays were called in Pri-fly and the results were seldom reversible.

Constant anticipation of unforeseen circumstances, human error, and new orders created extraordinary, 24-hour-a-day pressure on Midway's senior officers.

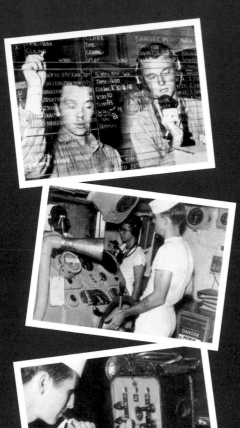

From keeping track of surface contacts to passing the word, Midway's bridge crew ensured their officers' commands were carried out precisely and promptly.

SIGHT UNSEEN

A 19-year-old once stood at Midway's helm, steering a 70,000-ton aircraft carrier by the numbers. Despite tiny portholes he had no view of the vast Pacific ahead off the bow. Nearby a phone talker relayed propulsion orders to other men stationed in front of throttle boards

deep inside the hull. The USS Midway succeeded like no other carrier because of something called "Midway Magic": an innate belief in a fellow sailor borne of rigorous training. The result was a culture of teamwork and team confidence that enabled the USS Midway to outperform every other carrier in the fleet during Operation Desert Storm.

Men checked navigation charts, relayed orders to the four engine rooms, and made recommendations to the officer of the deck regarding course and speed.

Underway replenishment was one of the most stressful and dangerous aspects of ship's operations.

FEEDING THE MIDWAY

The USS Midway sailed at the head of a massive relay race covering thousands of miles. A string of supply ships regularly pulled alongside to resupply the carrier, regardless of weather, time of day or sea state. In a sense, Midway was a hole in the water, swallowing massive amounts of consumables. The ship burned 100,000 gallons of fuel a day. The production of 1,000 loaves of bread consumed hundreds of pounds of flour. Sick bay needed x-ray film. The print shop consumed reams of paper. Stamps were the lifeblood of the post office. Engineering always needed replacement parts. Many Midway captains considered underway replenishment potentially more of a threat to the safety of Midway and its crew than combat operations.

Storing supplies below was a strenuous, all-hands effort.

LIFE AT SEA

A young man's eyes shine at the prospect of exploring Manilla, Mombasa, Yokosuka, the Mediterranean or the South China Sea. A few months later he's completed the Navy's boot camp at Great Lakes or San Diego and has learned the rudiments of his new rating or specialty. It is a whirlwind transformation from youngster into the rough form of a sailor.

Aboard the USS Midway, tens of thousands of young men crossed life's threshold into manhood. Chief Petty Officers, hard as shellac, molded them into men. Newly hatched sailors learned the essence of teamwork and the value of team spirit. "Old salts" alternately inspired and drove them toward self-discovery and growth.

In the end, more than 225,000 young men became adults on the decks of the USS Midway. Unending drills, duty that tested a man's grit, and the opportunity to explore faraway corners of the world became the guideposts by which Midway sailors first embraced and then extended the Magic of Midway.

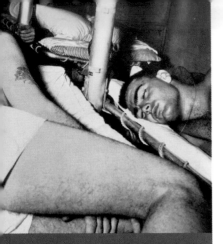

Exhausted sailors cherished
some shut-eye after a long
day at sea.

PRIVACY'S A DISTANT MEMORY

"Never sleep face to face with a man back from liberty. His beer breath can kill you." A man existed in a sea of men aboard the USS Midway. Early berths were four high, the topmost so confined a sailor couldn't turn over. Personal storage space was nearly nonexistent. A lack of air conditioning made talcum powder a cherished possession in the fight against rashes in Midway's early years. All this while Midway sometimes plunged 50 feet into oncoming seas, turning exhausted sailors green while trying to rest after 18 hours on duty.

Regardless of their rigorous
duties, the crew still found
the time and energy to get
together to "shoot the breeze."

Improved, more spacious
living quarters reflected
Midway's evolution from
a WWII warship to a
modern carrier.

Today, Midway's famous
mannequin, "Manny,"
demonstrates the close
quarters experienced by
the crew when cleaning up
after a hard day at sea.

A moment alone for personal contemplation was hard to find aboard a ship filled with 4,500 men.

ALONE AMONG THOUSANDS

Halfway around the world, a young sailor looks at his universe a little differently. Aboard the USS Midway, sailors stand ready to take aboard lines from a supply ship. The lines will support the fuel hoses used to resupply Midway on what seemed to many sailors an endless odyssey far from home.

Every job on Midway was important. A clean ship was a safer ship with fewer accidents and disease outbreaks.

The ship's hangar deck was almost always a busy place, day and night. Here, sailors organized newly arrived ordnance before storing it below.

Today, Midway's hangar bays echo with the sounds of guests coming
aboard to capture the essence of what made Midway Magic.

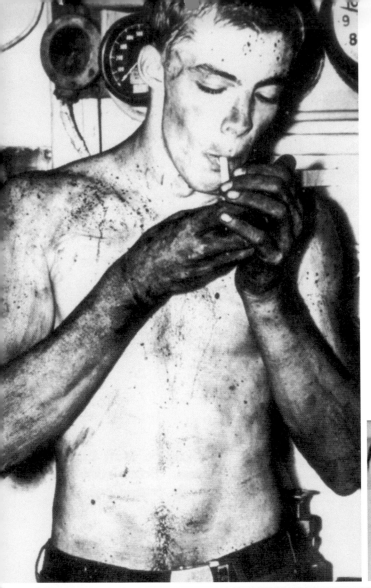

TOUGH DUTY

Steam was the life blood of the USS Midway and the engineering department its heart. Hundreds of young men completed brutal duties deep inside Midway. They scraped rust, tended dials, and repaired circuits. Together, they kept Midway's massive power plant generating 212,000 horsepower and enough electricity to supply the equivalent of one million homes in a land-based city. Grime and exhaustion often were the defining characteristics of engineering as young men worked behind the turbines and inside the boilers so that when the order for "flank speed" came, the USS Midway could bull its way through the ocean at better than 33 knots.

Midway's pilots rarely saw thousands of young men deep inside the ship's hull who scraped, scrubbed, and shined to exhaustion. Yet if these unsung heroes failed in their grimy and unglamorous jobs, Midway's ability to launch aircraft could be threatened.

Today, museum guests gather in the forecastle just as Midway's sailors once did for events ranging from graduation ceremonies to judicial proceedings.

BRAINS AND BRAWN

A sailor aboard Midway always had more than one responsibility. Although each member of the Midway team was highly trained in his specialty, there was often a need for brute strength to harness and direct the power of the ship's machinery to help meet Midway's mission. Men often were called on to lend a hand or a strong back. One moment a sailor might be rewiring one of Midway's 2,000 electrical motors and at the next he was ordered to join a working party stowing food and ammunition during an underway replenishment in the middle of the night. Brains and brawn never were in short supply aboard a huge aircraft carrier that required massive amounts of both.

Even aboard a modern aircraft carrier, some sailors learned ageless line-handling skills necessary for a number of ship's operations.

Sailors always looked for creative competition. Here, blindfolded boxers let it fly on the hangar deck during a "smoker."

Sometimes outrageous antics emerged when the flight deck served as "Steel Beach."

Being stuck aboard ship in a foreign port wasn't all bad if a sailor had a fishing pole handy.

LIFE AT SEA

Camaraderie and competition helped Midway sailors let off steam at sea. Poker, Bridge, Hearts, and Acey Deucy were played in berthing areas. Sometimes the shrill of a basketball referee's whistle filled the hangar deck. Smokers (boxing tournaments) were big hits among many sailors while others preferred the friendly solitude of fishing, rarely worrying about how they might haul a small shark 40 feet out of the water and up onto the sponson.

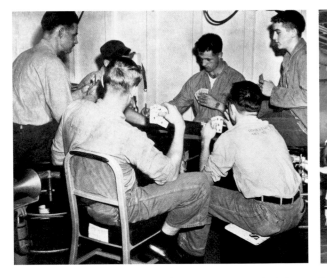

Some card games lasted weeks at a time, their players keeping close track of points and pots won and lost.

Intramural sports pitted division against division and encouraged competition among the ship's best athletes.

STAR STRUCK

The USS Midway sometimes caught the attention of Hollywood's biggest celebrities. As early as 1951 an entourage headed by Edward G Robinson and Lana Turner mesmerized the crew. In 1953, a Midway photographer's mate spotted starlet Brigitte Bardot (right) at the Cannes Film Festival. Bob Hope and his USO shows paid several visits to a jam-packed flight deck. In latter years, Tanya Tucker was a big hit and one of the most popular visiting celebrities was I Dream of Jeannie star Barbara Eden.

BIG 10 oz GLASS

Visit PEPSI-COLA
SERVICE MEN'S CENTER
NEW YORK CITY   WASHINGTON,
SAN FRANCISCO

The ship's "geedunk" was always a popular place for Midway sailors.
Sometimes lines of patient crewmen stretched through the hangar deck
when word spread that a new batch of ice cream was ready.

CROSSING THE LINE

Seagoing tradition framed life aboard Midway. BBQ smoke filled the air when the flight deck was idled. Sailors who crossed the equator the first time were initiated into the "Secret Society of Neptune Rex," transforming them from Pollywogs into Shellbacks after completing a frat house-style gauntlet of swats and swipes. Some Midway sailors qualified for the Order of the Blue Nose when the Navy ordered Midway north of the Arctic Circle in 1946 during Operation Frostbite.

Compliant "Pollywogs" get doused with concoctions of coffee grounds and hydraulic grease as part of their initiation into the Secret Society of Neptune Rex.

Thousands of men crossed the equator aboard Midway, enduring the longstanding tradition that turned them into trusted Shellbacks.

When in port, the hangar deck was converted into a place of worship, ringing with the voices of men united in song and prayer.

PERSPECTIVE

A Cold War, combat, and the rise of terrorism forced Midway sailors to occasionally serve above and beyond the call of duty. Sometimes monotonous, sometimes dangerous duty frequently was haunted by the unexpected. More than 200 men lost their lives aboard Midway. Many sailors sought perspective and personal answers during Midway's religious ceremonies. Multi-denominational chaplains presided over funerals, Sunday services, and religion-specific rites and ceremonies.

Flight elevators, hangar bays, the forecastle, and even a small compartment under a galley offered sanctuary for officers and crew when a Midway chaplain gathered the men for personal reflection at sea.

Taps, the last call in a sailor's life, sometimes marked the final salute to a fallen comrade.

ON THE ROOF

Massive jets thunder off the bow, rocketing from 0 to 150 knots in 268 feet. Further aft, one plane after another is slamming onto the flight deck, the pilots desperate to hook one of three arresting wires in an area the size of a tennis court. "If my fillings aren't yanked out immediately by my aircraft grabbing a wire, I go full throttle without even thinking about it to get back off the deck," one of them said.

The USS Midway's 4.2-acre flight deck (called the "roof" by the men who toiled there) was a cacophony of screaming aircraft and pantomiming personnel who looked alien in their gear and who were battered by a steady 30-knot wind across the deck. It was an environment of daring and danger like no other on earth, an environment in which aviators placed their lives in the hands of catapult and arresting gear operators, jet engine mechanics, shooters, "grapes," and "ordies."

TAKING TO THE AIR

The F-4 Phantom growls in anticipation of freedom. More than a dozen men scurry around wing tips and wheels, locking it onto the shuttle that soon will race down the catapult before slamming into an unseen water brake tank near the bow. A man, his face hidden by tinted goggles, stands on the deck-edge catwalk. His eyes sweep across the choreographed ballet on the rough flight deck.

High above in the island's pri-fly, the Air Boss, too, scans the flight deck, monitoring the foul line, glancing aft toward the landing signal officers. The illuminated "ball" on the far side of the deck catches his eye as Midway's bow crests a swell and sea spray dances down the deck on the headwind.

Countless hours of training and drills by hundreds of men in dozens of specialties have led to this moment. The shooter on the catwalk is ready to press the button that will fire the catapult, ready to send USS Midway aviators into the sky to patrol, to fight, to protect lives, and to return to the safety of the flight deck.

The "shooter" presses the button that accelerates an aircraft from 0 to 170 miles an hour in just over two seconds.

Today, an F-4 Phantom jet sits poised on one of Midway's catapults, ready to carry out mission orders from the bridge.

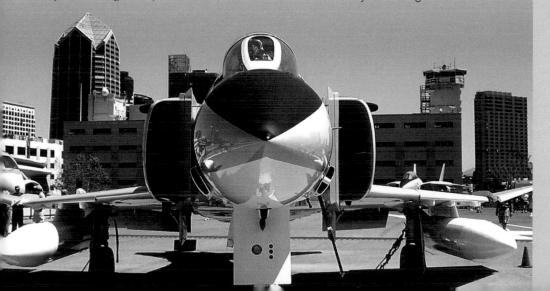

41

A Midway jet breaks free of the catapult's bridle as it slams down onto the flight deck extension. This catapult system later was replaced by the more modern "nose tow" system.

Pilots and crew celebrate another milestone landing on Midway's always-busy flight deck.

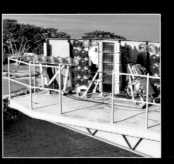

The fresnel lens stands ready to guide another pilot to a safe landing while launch operations take place forward off the bow.

SEAKEEPING

Battleship-inspired design elements made the Midway class unique among carriers. Top-heavy the day she was launched at 45,000 tons, the USS Midway became famous for rolling in even moderate seas. In heavy weather, waves often crashed onto her deck, 50 feet above the ocean surface. It's said that some Navy aviators were qualified to land on every carrier in the fleet except the USS "Rock 'n Roll." For all her quirks, after nearly 47 years, Midway remained one of the most nimble carriers in the fleet when she was decommissioned at a hefty 70,000 tons in 1992.

Midway was infamous for taking water over the bow, forcing the catapult officer to time launches between torrents of ocean.

Shipboard cartoonists depicted some of the problems encountered by Midway pilots landing aboard a pitching flight deck.

Sailors wore jacket patches celebrating Midway's famous ability to "out-roll" other aircraft carriers in heavy seas.

Today, Midway's bridge still sports Navy awards for its flight operations, engineering, damage control, weapons and deck division.

The U.S. Navy often tasked Midway with experimental operations. One day Midway sailors were stunned to see a blimp on final approach to the flight deck.

FLIGHT DECK BALLET

Perched precariously over the water on the ship's port quarter, the landing signal officer (LSO) stood a lonely vigil helping pilots maintain the proper speed and altitude necessary for a safe landing aboard Midway. One of the best pilots on the ship, an LSO's directions made the difference between a successful landing and a fiery crash on the carrier's flight deck.

In the end, it was an LSO's instincts, fortified by hundreds of successful landings as a pilot, that served as guides when he brought each pilot aboard. Naval aviators who earned their qualifications or completed a safe deployment aboard Midway owed a large debt of gratitude to the LSOs who stood their posts in all weather conditions.

Today, the LSO is assisted by a closed-circuit television system that monitors approaching aircraft.

In Midway's early days, the LSO used hand-held paddles during the day and wore a specially lighted suit at night. Later, as technology advanced, he had audio and visual aids to help bring a pilot safely aboard. The LSO was especially important on Midway because the carrier's unique seakeeping characteristics sometimes produced a flight deck pitching pattern rarely seen on other carriers.

TRAINING AND LUCK

Coming in too low, an aircraft slammed into the aft end of the flight deck, also called the round-down, splitting the plane in two.

The decapitated cockpit and nose slid down the deck, racing ahead of an expanding ball of fire. Note the sailors hiding behind the ship's antenna (bottom left) as the inferno approaches.

Firefighting crews quickly extinguished the flight deck blaze as emergency personnel gathered around the wreckage.

Incredibly, the pilot walked away from this 1951 crash in a scorched flight suit and with minor injuries.

Today, visitors from around the world fill Midway's flight deck, exploring aircraft, entering helicopters, and climbing up into the island to experience the command "Magic" on the bridge and in primary flight control.

A NATIONAL RESOURCE

The San Diego Aircraft Carrier Museum aboard the USS Midway is well on its way to becoming a flagship floating naval aviation museum where visitors "Live the Adventure, Honor the Legend" of Midway's odyssey. Most days the museum also is host to private evening

events and in its first year was named the nation's "Event Venue of the Year" by a national meeting planner organization. The museum's education and youth overnight programs make it an invaluable resource for generations to come.

Education programs, special events, community ceremonies, and youth overnight programs comprise the hive of activity that is aboard Midway. Students, guests, residents and visitors all are eager for the opportunity to learn what it was like to live, work, and complete a mission aboard the nation's longest-serving aircraft carrier.

CHAPTER FIVE

Pilots from Midway's air wing escort a Russian reconnaissance aircraft well clear of Midway, somewhere in the Pacific.

IN HARM'S WAY

The USS Midway's first captain was visibly disappointed when the carrier was commissioned on Sept. 10, 1945. WWII was over so he would not lead his new ship into battle to teach America's enemies a lesson. Yet over the next 47 years the USS Midway sailed into harm's way time and again as she answered her nation's call.

Midway steamed a 47-year odyssey that spanned the use of WWII-era Hellcats and the F-18 Hornets of Operation Desert Storm. It was an odyssey that saw a Cold War erupt, stagnate, and die through confrontations with Communist Russia and China. The Cuban Missile Crisis, Vietnam, an Iranian hostage crisis, and the liberation of Kuwait were all mile markers in Midway's unmatched voyage almost to the doorstep of the 21st century.

Landmark sorties included the downing of the first MiG of the Vietnam War and the last MiG eight years later. Other missions carried the potential of war when Midway aviators scrambled to meet incoming Russian bombers in nerve-wracking games of chicken. Countless missions were planned, aircraft readied and their crews poised, waiting for another call for Midway Magic.

A Russian aircraft never got this close to Midway without a Midway fighter escort during a Cold War era filled with unpublicized showdowns over the horizon in the Pacific.

A Midway signalman hoists a flag celebrating two kills by the ship's air wing.

FACING THE ENEMY

While an aircraft carrier task group's presence might give enemies a moment of pause, sometimes the ultimate mission was to take the war to an enemy. In Vietnam, Midway's pilots flew several combat missions a day, frequently braving the "Iron Triangle," a heavily fortified area of North Vietnam. Constrictive rules of engagement often hamstrung Midway's pilots as they dodged surface-to-air missiles and scanned the sky for approaching enemy aircraft on their way to and from a target.

BADGES OF DANGER

A pilot rode the tail of an enemy aircraft until he heard the low growl of his weapon system locking onto the enemy. At the press of a button, a heat-seeking missile rocketed away from his aircraft which already was flying nearly at the speed of sound. Whether the missile destroyed its target depended upon the skill of the Midway pilot hundreds of miles away from the carrier over enemy territory. After disengaging, he faced a life-threatening gauntlet as he made his way back to the safety of Midway's flight deck.

Midway aircraft sometimes limped back home with massive battle damage. More than one Midway pilot had to bail out of his dying aircraft over the

ocean and hope that American search-and-rescue personnel would reach him before coastal enemy patrol boats arrived on the scene.

The awards earned by the USS Midway reflect the courage of her sailors as they served in four major conflicts over more than four decades.

Midway's newspaper poked fun at one of the hazards of sailing above the Arctic Circle in winter.

FLYING AMONG THE ICEBERGS

In 1946 a ravaged world stood at the dawn of the Cold War. Pentagon planners feared WWIII might begin in the frozen North if relations with Russia soured and an invasion of Europe was launched through Scandinavia.

WWII had been mostly a warm-water war. Russia had military bases above the Arctic Circle while the U.S. Navy's bases were in more moderate climates. It was left to the newly commissioned USS Midway to teach the Navy how to fly among the icebergs. In March 1946 the steel-decked carrier sailed north toward Greenland and was the first of its type to operate extensively in winter north of the Arctic Circle. Midway sailors learned what it took to keep exposed aircraft in flying condition and a flight deck ready for air operations.

WEAPONS

From the day she was commissioned, the USS Midway could deliver huge amounts of ordnance. She sailed at the dawn of the nuclear age. In fact, the Midway was the first American carrier large enough to launch the massive Neptunes and Savages that carried nuclear weapons. By the late 1940s Midway carried nearly 10 percent of the nation's nuclear arsenal as it sailed the Mediterranean, protecting NATO's southern flank in the early years of the Cold War. Had Midway's aviators been ordered to launch with nuclear weapons, it would have been a one-way trip. Midway's straight deck wasn't large enough for those planes to land. More than 40 years later her ordnance crews were still loading machine guns, arming 500-pound bombs, and tending classified ordnance of massive force.

This non-descript "closet" was a vigorously guarded entrance to Midway's nuclear weapons storage and maintenance facilities.

Museum visitors see the 500-pound bombs where they were assembled on the mess deck, alongside rows of men having lunch or dinner.

A flight deck ordnanceman installs a fuse in the nose of a "thousand pounder" as an aircraft is prepared for the next strike.

OPERATION FREQUENT WIND

Midway's humanitarian missions nearly equalled her combat deployments. As South Vietnam fell on April 30, 1975, Midway led the rescue effort when Armed Forces Radio played the secret "go order," I'm Dreaming of a White Christmas. More than 3,000 refugees, many of them instant orphans as parents tossed children aboard departing helicopters, flew out to Midway in a tidal wave of flights over the next two days. Midway sailors were stunned when they opened a helo cargo door and pulled 80 children out of a space intended to carry 12 Marines. The youngsters

had been stacked like kindling for the flight toward an unknown future. That night, the children slept in berths and bunks vacated by the ship's crew and even on bubble wrap on the hangar deck.

Operation Frequent Wind was emblematic of several humanitarian missions completed by Midway, some of them high profile, others less well known yet equally poignant. Midway Magic saved thousand of lives the world over.

From pioneering search-and-rescue missions in the 1940s to humanitarian and anti-submarine warfare missions in the 1990s, helicopters aboard Midway reflected the evolution of the helicopter's role and its contribution to naval aviation.

The ship's missile crews were responsible for ensuring two sophisticated Air Sparrow launchers were ready for action 24 hours a day.

Midway's pioneering V-2 success set the stage for the development and deployment of supersonic air-to-air missiles later used by Midway's air wing.

THE DAWN OF NAVAL MISSILE WARFARE

A Flash Gordon-esque rocket rumbled off the USS Midway's flight deck on Sept. 6, 1947. The crew held its collective breath as the captured German V-2 rocket belched yellow flame before it lifted off the flight deck, tilted to one side, and then narrowly missed the island. Seconds later it was detonated before it hit the USS Knox that was steaming alongside. Minutes later Midway's airborne air wing returned safely to the two-year-old carrier. Operation Sandy conducted off Bermuda answered the question of whether ships could withstand the thrust of a rocket launch. It was one of many instances in which the USS Midway was the first to cross a technological or operational threshold, leading the U.S. Navy into new waters.

Alarm spread through Midway sailors when a captured German V-2 rocket went off course almost immediately after takeoff during Operation Sandy in 1947. Although it had to be quickly detonated, Midway proved a ship could withstand the thrust of a rocket launch. It marked the dawn of naval missile warfare.

Scientists prepare the world's first ship-launch missile flight from Midway's flight deck.

CHAPTER SIX

Each of Midway's four
propellers weighs 22 tons and
measures 18 feet across.

ENGINEERING MARVEL

The USS Midway stunned the world when commissioned on Sept. 10, 1945. The extraordinary engineering feat was matched by its massiveness. Midway was the first ship in the world too large for the Panama Canal, and would be the largest ship in the world until the USS Forrestal was commissioned in 1955. Her statistics were numbing: more than 1,750 compartments, an estimated 1,500 telephones, more than 3,000 miles of copper conductor, 12 boilers feeding 4 turbines that required 260 gallons of fuel per mile. Her four propellers each spanned 18 feet and weighed 22 tons. More than 1,000 men were required in Engineering to keep propulsion, desalinization, electrical, electronic, communications, steel infrastructure and plumbing systems operational while at sea.

Today, the equipment stands idle, the men who served the machinery now gone. School children study physics and chemistry, using the equipment that once drove Midway through the seas.

Main control (above) and one of four throttle boards (top) were two of the links between the captain's orders given on the bridge and Midway's massive propulsion system, an engineering marvel at the close of WWII.

Midway's massive size dwarfed its 20-ton anchors as shipyard workers gaze up at the drydocked behemoth. The USS Midway was the first ship too large to sail through the Panama Canal.

SEAGOING GOLIATH

During her 47 years of service, the USS Midway grew well beyond her original dimensions as her peacekeeper role expanded. When launched in 1945, the carrier measured 968 feet long with a flight deck of 924 feet. She was 136 feet wide and weighed in at just over 60,000 tons fully loaded, including 332,000 gallons of aviation fuel. Center-deck elevators could lift 26,000 pounds of Corsairs and Hellcats up to the flight deck.

By 1990, Midway had grown to just over 1,000 feet in length. One of the shafts from turbine to propeller was 1.5 football fields long. She sported an angled deck and an extreme width that had nearly doubled to 258 feet. Her displacement had increased to 69,000 tons, in part to accommodate aviation fuel capacity that had quadrupled to 1.2 million gallons. Hydraulic catapults had been replaced by steam-powered "cats" while her relocated aircraft elevator capacity had increased fourfold to 110,000 pounds worth of Intruders, Hawkeyes and Hornets.

Each Midway anchor weighs 20 tons. A single anchor chain link weighs 130 pounds.

THE CREW

Midway's commissioning crew in 1945 consisted of 316 officers and 3,127 enlisted men. By 1990, the ship's crew had increased 35 percent in order to maintain the ship's state-of-the-art systems. As Midway was modernized, new skills and greater teamwork were required. Boatswain's Mates manned the ship's decks and stood watch. Quartermasters navigated through trackless seas while Enginemen and Electrician's Mates maintained the ship's power plant and electrical distribution systems. Interior Communications and Electronics Technicians, tended electronics, communications, radar, and navigation systems.

In the Combat Information Center, Radarmen and Air Traffic Controllers manned computer consoles and status boards detecting, identifying, and controlling ship and aircraft movements. Meteorological Teams and Photographic Interpreters prepared briefings for pilots while Ship's Servicemen, Hull Technicians, Fire Control Technicians, and thousands of others worked around the clock in a marathon of tightly choreographed teamwork to keep the ship ready to meet the next call to duty.

A MIRACLE OF COMPLEXITIES

Midway originally had 59 anti-aircraft guns ringing its flight deck.

Midway answered the call of nine U.S. presidents, from Harry Truman to George Bush

High-pressure steam (up to 600 pounds per square inch) was the lifeblood of Midway and extremely dangerous.

Midway was the first American aircraft carrier featuring a steel flight deck.

The top of Midway's mast is more than 200 feet above the water.

Each Midway anchor weighs 20 tons.

Midway was built in about two years and cost $90 million in 1945.

Midway's flight deck rises 50 feet above the water.

Midway held 3.4 million gallons of ship and aviation fuel. Refueling took place every 6 to 8 days.

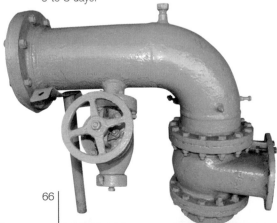

Midway's arresting system could bring a 50,000-pound aircraft to a stop in less than 3 seconds.

Midway's flight and hangar decks are speckled with more than 4,000 padeyes used to tie down aircraft and equipment.

Midway's keel was 33 feet below the water.

Midway's 3,000 emergency lights would come to life in the event of a power failure.

CV41 stands for (C) Carrier (V) fixed wing (41) forty-first carrier planned.

Pilots landing aboard Midway had to touch down in an area about the size of a tennis court.

Ship designers once considered installing a catapult inside Midway to launch aircraft out the side of the ship.

Midway is longer than three football fields, end to end.

Midway produced enough electricity to supply 1 million homes.

CAUTION HEARING PROTECTION MUST BE WORN IN THIS AREA

Many sailors were limited to four-hour duty watches deep inside Midway due to excessive noise and temperatures that often reached 120°

More than 225,000 men served aboard the USS Midway.

Midway's signal flags are a Navy tradition dating back to an era of wooden ships and primitive communications.

Midway's massive power plant produced 212,000 horsepower.

Officers and men of the airwings aboard Midway wore patches to identify their squadrons. These badges of honor were standardized and registered by the office of the Chief of Naval Operations.

THE FINAL MISSION

The sun rises on San
Diego and Midway,
marking a new era
in the carrier's
unmatched history.

The ex-USS Midway has embarked on its final mission to become the nation's flagship floating naval aviation museum and a world-renowned education center and tribute to service, sacrifice and honor. How fitting it is that Midway is located in San Diego, California, the birthplace of naval aviation where daring men pioneered flight over water nearly 100 years ago.

Dynamic hands-on exhibits and educational activities, coupled with an interactive and engaging staff, enable Midway to transcend its World War II roots to become a 21st century vanguard of vigilance, perseverance, and duty in an uncertain world.

Live the Adventure,
Honor the Legend

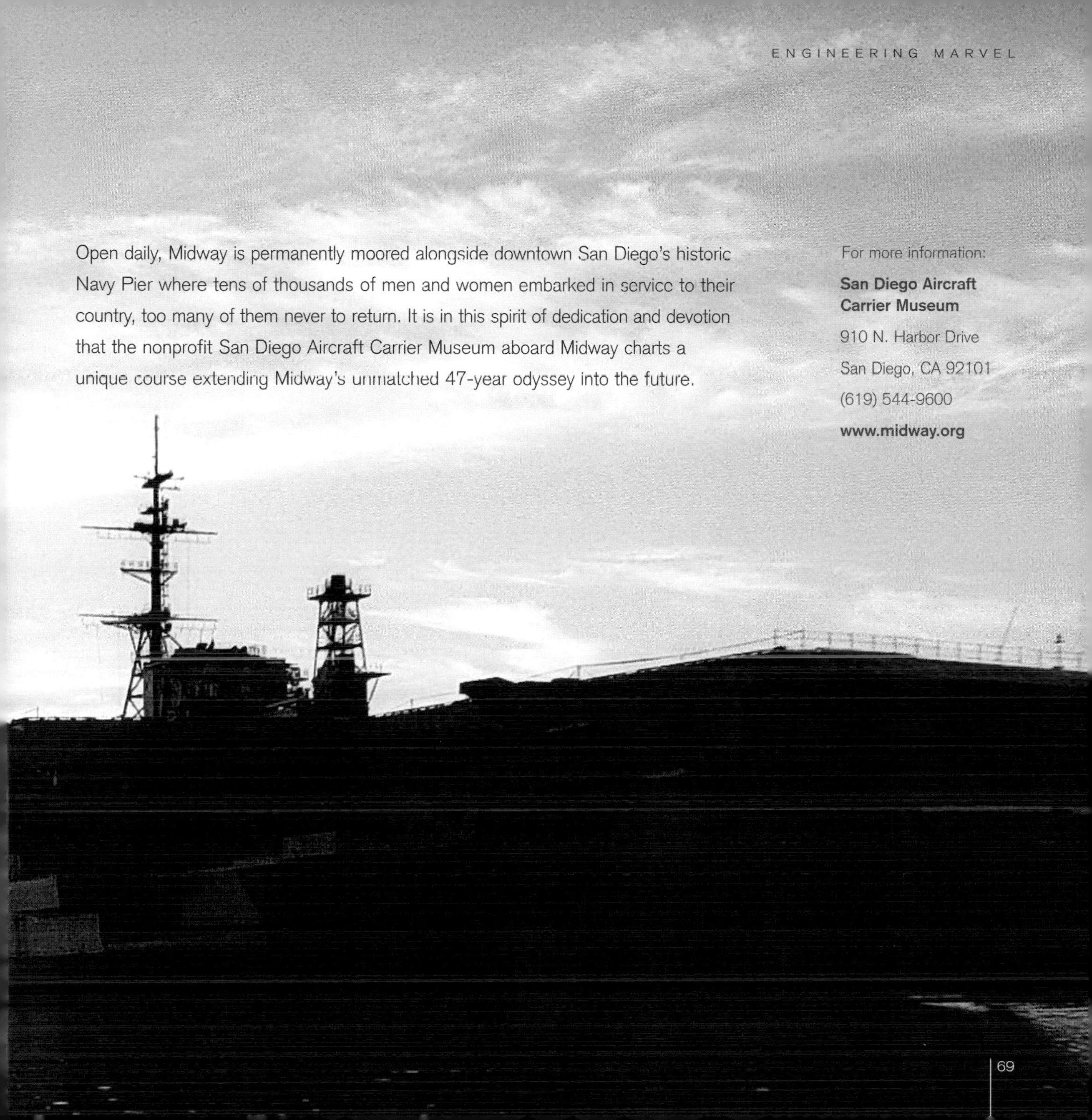

Open daily, Midway is permanently moored alongside downtown San Diego's historic Navy Pier where tens of thousands of men and women embarked in service to their country, too many of them never to return. It is in this spirit of dedication and devotion that the nonprofit San Diego Aircraft Carrier Museum aboard Midway charts a unique course extending Midway's unmatched 47-year odyssey into the future.

For more information:

San Diego Aircraft Carrier Museum

910 N. Harbor Drive

San Diego, CA 92101

(619) 544-9600

www.midway.org

A 47-YEAR ODYSSEY

1945

The USS Midway is the largest ship in the world when commissioned on September 10. At 45,000 tons, she dwarfs the Essex class carriers of WWII.

1947

Midway launches the first missile (a captured German V-2 rocket) at sea in 1947 during Operation Sandy off the coast of Bermuda.

MIDWAY

1946

During Operation Frostbite in 1946, Midway aviators teach the rest of the Navy how to fly among the icebergs in below-freezing temperatures.

1973

In 1973 Midway becomes the first U.S. carrier to be forward-deployed in a foreign country, calling Yokosuka, Japan home for the next 18 years.

2004

On June 7, 2004 Midway begins its final deployment as the San Diego Aircraft Carrier Museum. She serves as a permanent tribute, memorial, and education center of naval aviation and service to country.

MAGIC

Midway
M A G I C

San Diego Aircraft Carrier Museum
910 N. Harbor Drive
San Diego, CA 92101
(619) 544-9600

www.midway.org

1975

Midway plays a key role in the miraculous evacuation of more than 3,000 refugees when South Vietnam falls to the communists in 1975.

1991

Midway serves as a flagship for naval air operations during Desert Storm in 1991. She outperforms other carriers even though the USS Midway is the oldest and smallest in the fleet.

MIDWAY MEMORIES

Scott McGaugh   Rudy Shappee
scott@midwaymagic.com   rtshappee@cox.net
(858) 229-7811   (619) 286-8689

Book design by Jo-Lin Govek
ChampCohen Design Associates
Del Mar, California
www.champcohen.com

Printed in Hong Kong.

Photographs courtesy of Kristen Peelle,
San Diego Aircraft Carrier Museum

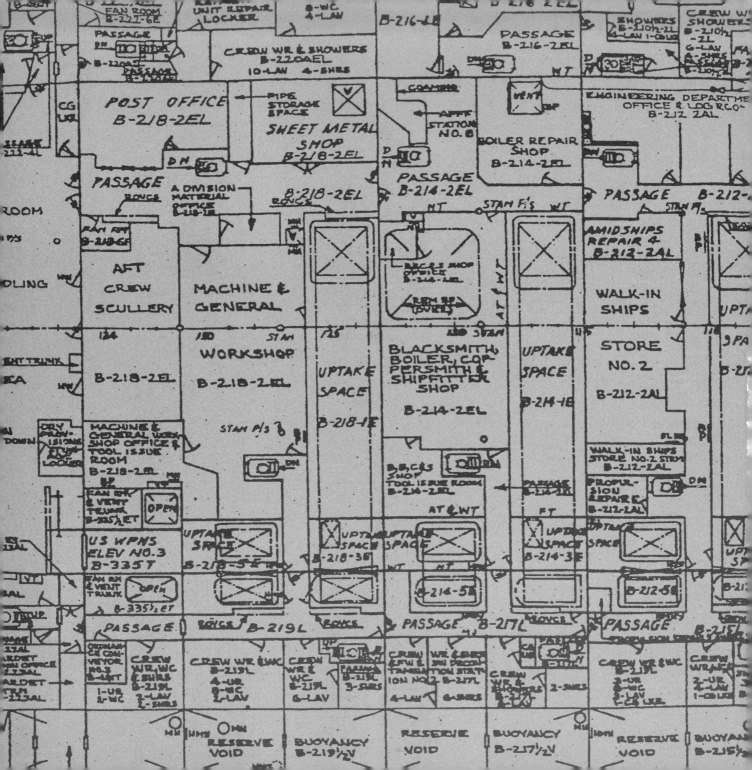